Ajeeb Dastaan Hai Yeh

The tale of unspoken love

Pranav K Solanky

BookLeaf Publishing
India | USA | UK

Made with ❤ on the BookLeaf Publishing Platform
www.bookleafpub.in
www.bookleafpub.com

Dedication

To the old diary pages, unanswered messages and that one photo I never deleted.

Preface

There are stories that never leave the lips, only the eyes. There are names that live quietly in prayers, but not in conversations. This book is about love - the one that was never confessed, but always felt. It is about walking beside someone in silence, lighting up their world while burning quietly in your own. It's about the letter never sent and glances that stayed a second too long.

These poems were written in moments of stillness - between letting go and holding on, between loving someone and learning to love myself. "Ajeeb daastaan hai yeh" is not just a title. It is a question that echoes in the hearts of all those who gave everything, and asked for nothing. If you ever loved someone, smiled through pain, or found yourself in the process of losing someone - this book is yours.

Acknowledgements

Every word in this book was born from a feeling, but it found its way to paper because of the people who stood beside me – in silence, in chaos, and in kindness.

First, my deepest gratitude to Dad and Mom – the quiet pillars of my life. Thank you for never asking me to "get over it" or "write something happy." Your unwavering support gave me the freedom to feel deeply, write honestly, and chase emotions others were too afraid to touch. You let me pour my heart into words, even when it meant seeing your child ache. That's a kind of love I will never be able to repay – only honour, in everything I create.

To my sisters – thank you for being my built-in best friends. For reading my verses before anyone else, for sending me "this one's my favourite" messages, and for believing I was meant for something greater – even when I was buried in doubt. You remind me, always, that I am more than my heartbreak.

To my friends – both near and far, old and new – thank you for standing beside the poet and the person. To Aprameya, Ravinder, Dhun and Diya – you deserve a special mention, because you listened to every poem, every rant, and every silence without once asking "Itna sad kyun likhta hai?" That quiet acceptance, that space to just be — that's rare. And it made this book possible.

To my mentors, teachers, and those anonymous faces who told me to "keep writing" when I shared verses online or at a mic — your words stayed longer than you'll ever know.

To the strangers who became readers, the readers who became believers — thank you for letting my sadness sit next to yours.

And finally, to her.

The one who inspired it all without knowing.

You were never mine — and perhaps that's what made every line possible.

No, I won't name you. That's between me, the stars, and these pages.

But thank you — for being the poem I could never finish.

1. The beginning: Falling in love

When I saw her for the first time, in the crowd. It was just for a minute, but something changed forever. I started going every day to the same spot, waiting for her to come and this is when I wrote -

Woh pehli nazar ka kasoor ya dil ka koi fasana
Ek lamhe main kho gaya hu, iss dil ka ab na koi thikana
Chupchap dekhta raha usse jaise koi khwab pura hua
Woh muskurayi aur yu laga mera har dard dur hua
Magar yeh lamha teher na saka, haqeekat se takraya
Main bus dekhta reh gaya, aur woh bheed main kho gaya
Ab har shaam main ussi mod pe apna kinara lagata hu
Shayad phir mile issi khayaal main duba rehta hu

2

This poem is during a breezy afternoon - when I spoke to her for the first time.We spoke nothing too deep, just a light conversation. but while she talked, I was somewhere else entirely. The way her dupatta danced in the wind, brushing past me like a secret, the way she smiled while tucking her hair behind her ear — I was mesmerized. Words were being exchanged, but I was busy falling.

Hawa se uska dupatta
Khushbu ke saath mere paas aaya
Kabhi chera chupa gaya
Toh kabhi dil behla gaya
Kabhi lehra kar mhujse uljha
Toh kabhi baahon ko chukar nikal gaya
Woh sambhalti rahi muskurakar
Aur main bus usse dekhta reh gaya

3

She became the moon in my sky – always a little out of reach, but somehow still the center of everything. And I was the quiet night, wrapping myself around her light, hoping she'd notice the way I stayed. She never really knew, but I felt everything with her

Tu chaand hai toh main raat huya
Tere bina bhi main tere saath huya
Teri khushi main hasta raha
Tere gham main udaas hua

4

This poem was written as an answer to a simple question: *"Tum mere liye kya kar sakte ho?"* It's a boy telling the girl – I may not move mountains, but I'll walk every step with you, love you through every breath, and quietly wish for your joy, even if I'm not the one beside you.

Zameen se aasman tak ka safar tera hoga
Har ek kadam main tu mere saath hoga
Dil ki har dhadkan tera naam gayegi
Aur meri har dua teri khushiyaan sajayegi

5

Friends began to complain, "*Tu aur kuch karta bhi hai kya?*" But how do you explain to them that when someone becomes your entire world, even silence starts to sound like their name? I wasn't obsessed – just deeply, helplessly in love. And no matter what the world said, my heart had made its choice.

Uski hi yaadon main kho jaate hai
Uske khayaalon main jee jaate hai
Duniya kuch bhi kahe kya farq padta hai
Hum toh sirf usse chahte hai

6. Realisation

I saw her, but the laughing freely with someone else - and it hit like fire in the chest. It wasn't jealousy, just a quiet heartbreak.. watching the one you love smile in a world where you no longer exist, its a feeling I can't describe.

Teri yaadon main har raat kat jaati hai
Dil ki baat labon tak nahi aati hai
Tu hasta hai kisi aur ke sang waha
Aur yaha mere seene main aag lag jaati hai.

7

Since childhood, I always believed that love meant madness, intensity, something straight out of the movies. But growing up taught me otherwise,

Ab hum kya kare,
Humne toh bachpan se suna tha Ishq main junoon hota hai
Ab jaana hai ye toh sirf adhuri duaon ka sukoon hota hai

8

Even moon feels like a friend who understands your heartbreak. I used to watch it linger near her window, just like my thoughts did - but this time I spoke to it, like an old companion, I said

Chaand dheere dheere therne laga
Uski khidki pe aakar baithne laga
Main haskar bola - 'Chodna yaar
Woh kisi aur ki hai tu kyu behekne laga'

9

This poem was born the day she came to me, eyes glowing, asking if I could help her get closer to someone she liked. And I? I stood there, heart quietly shattering, yet nodding with a smile. I walked beside her, laid down every comfort, and burned silently in the background while she laughed with someone else. Even when I saw her hand in his, I chose to smile – not because it didn't hurt, but because her happiness mattered more than my heartbreak. That's what unspoken love looks like – choosing their joy, even when it breaks you.

Teri raahon main phool bichake main khud kaaton pe chala hu m
Tu jiske saath hasti rahi main usse dekh kar jala hu
Aaj tera haath kisi aur ke haath main dekhkar bhi muskurata hu
Teri khushi main apni mohabbat roz bhulata hu

10

This one came from the part of my story I rarely talk about — the part where I became the bridge between her and the one she loved. She never knew how much it cost me to make that happen. I brought them together, helped their story bloom, all while hiding my own chapters. I told myself I'd move on, that I'd forget her, that I'd laugh like it didn't ache. But no matter how much I tried to bury her name, it kept beating inside my chest. I became the light in her path by burning myself down — and even then, I couldn't bring myself to stop loving her.

Teri raahon main jalte diye bankar, khud ko raakh kar diya
Teri khushi main apna gham chupa, har lamha muskurata gaya
Aaj bhi tera naam dil se mita nahi paya
Teri khushi ke liye Khud hi khud ko samjha nahi paya

11. Breaking point

This poem came from that breaking point – the moment I realized that no matter how much love I gave, I'd never belong in her world. I had carved every corner of my life with her name, dreamt of a future that only I believed in. But when her world had no space for me, I had to make the hardest choice – to erase my own story. It wasn't just about letting go of her... it was about burning down the version of myself that only existed because of her. Some goodbyes aren't spoken – they're written in ashes.

Har raah pe tera naam likhne chale the
Par apni hi kahani mitani padi.
Teri duniya mein jagah na mili jab mujhe,
Toh khud ki duniya jalaani padi

12

There comes a point in love where the weight of memories becomes heavier than the moments themselves. I had climbed this mountain of hope, chasing beauty, chasing her — like one chases the view of a distant waterfall. But the higher I climbed, the lonelier it felt. The moon, once my silent companion in sleepless nights, now hides behind clouds, ashamed of witnessing my descent. Her absence echoed so loudly in my heart that even the heights I once sought now feel like edges I could fall from — not because I want to end it all, but because the fall promises stillness... something my restless heart craves.

Chaand bhi ab shaayad sharmane laga hai,
Teri yaadon ka bojh mujhpe bhadane laga hai.
Jharne ki khoobsurti dekhne jo chadha tha,
Ab usi unchai se girne ko dil chaahne laga hai.

13

After she left, something within me dimmed – not with drama, but like a quiet sunset over an abandoned city. Everything I once was felt hollow, like empty streets echoing with old laughter and forgotten dreams. Most of my heart turned into silence, like a town without its people. And yet, one small corner of it still burns – not with hope, but with the flame of her memories. A soft, persistent fire that refuses to die, lighting up the emptiness with nothing but the past.

Tere jaane ke baad main yu badal gaya
Jaise khaali se sheher main suraj dhal gaya
Dil ka teen chothai hissa khaali hai
Bus ek kona teri yaadon se jal gaya

14

There are phases when emotions lose their meaning – when you laugh without reason and cry without warning. I found myself trapped in such a phase, lost in the maze of someone's memories. She was right there, so close that I could hear her laugh, feel her presence... and yet, something had changed. The distance wasn't physical, it was emotional – like a wall made of silence. I wanted to speak, to reach out, to hold on. But my words always stopped at the edge of my lips, swallowed by fear, pride, or perhaps the understanding that some things are never meant to be said out loud.

Bewajah haste the bewajah ro pade
Kisi ki yaadon mai hum yunhi kho gaye
Woh paas hoke bhi dur ho gayi
Hum chah ke bhi kuch keh na sake

15

Some names are too sacred to be spoken. I never said hers aloud, but she lived in every silent prayer. I knew she belonged to someone else, yet my heart never let her go. Some people remain – not in life, but in the spaces we never fully heal.

Tera naam zubaan tak laaya nahi
Par thuje kabhi apni duaon se bhulaya nahi
Tu kisi aur ki thi ye pata hai mhuje
Phir bhi thuje dil se nikala nahi

16

Every evening feels like diving into a sea of her memories – familiar, overwhelming, and impossible to escape. I wear a smile for the world, but inside, something breaks a little more each day. I still talk to her in my head, replaying every word she once said. I had asked for her in my prayers, and now... I only ask for the strength to stay away.

Teri yaadon ka dariya hai, har shaam isme doobta hu
Muskurata hu duniya ke saamne, magar andar se roz toothta hu
Teri har baat ko sochkar khud hi se baatein karta hu
Thuje maanga tha duaon main, ab tum se hi faasle rakhta hu

17. Acceptance

There comes a moment when even the heart, after all its rebellion, learns to whisper reason to itself. I used to find hope in the moonlight resting on her window, like some silent promise. But now, I smile and remind myself – she's no longer mine to long for. It's not bitterness, just acceptance. A quiet conversation with my own heart, asking it to finally let go.

Chaand dheere dheere therne laga
Teri khidki pe aakar baithne laga
Main haskar bola "chodna yaar
Woh kisi aur ki hai tu kyu behekne laga"

18

Sometimes, love feels like a beautiful traveler who stops at your doorstep just for a while – not to stay, but to rest. I loved her with everything I had, but I was never her destination. I was just a path she crossed, unknowingly leaving behind memories like footprints in the dust. And now, I watch her walk toward her true journey, while I stay behind, learning how to be nothing more than a passing moment in someone else's story.

Jisse chaha tha woh kisi aur ki manzil thi
Main toh ek rasta tha jaha se woh sirf guzri thi

19

They say "*Ishq toh aag ka dariya hai, doob ke jaana hai*" – and I never understood it until I fell. Love wasn't just about warmth and passion; it was about burning silently while smiling. This poem is born from that fire – where drowning isn't the end, but the beginning of a quiet survival. Ishq toh woh dariya hai jisme doobna zaruri hai, because only by drowning do we truly understand its depth. And sometimes, we emerge not whole, but alive – carrying the weight of memories like scars we learn to wear with grace.

Ishq toh woh dariya hai jisme doobna zaruri hai
Aur kabhi kabhi doobkar zinda rehna majboori hai

20

There comes a point in every one-sided love story where letting go becomes the only act of self-love left. This poem captures that quiet surrender – not of feelings, but of the pain that came with holding on. *Ab chod diya maine khwaab sajana* is not about forgetting her, but about choosing peace over longing. It's the moment when you stop waiting at doors that were never meant to open for you, and decide to walk away – not because the love is gone, but because you finally chose yourself.

Ab chod diya maine khwaab sajana
Jo mera tha hi nahi usse apna banana
Mohabbat thi, aur shayad rahegi bhi
Par ab na uss galiyon se guzarna aur khud ko rulana

21

Her words helped me forget my sorrows, and her memories made my lonely journey feel alive. She was never truly mine—just a beautiful illusion—but that very illusion made me a poet, giving my heart a voice through my verses.

Uski baaton ne har gham ko bhula diya
Uske yaadon ne tanha safar saja diya
Woh meri thi, ya shayad meri khushfehmi thi
Par uss khushfehmi ne mhuje shayaar bana diya

www.ingramcontent.com/pod-product-compliance
Lightning Source LLC
Chambersburg PA
CBHW070654240926
51846CB00003BA/917
* 9 7 8 9 3 7 1 5 6 9 0 6 4 *